QUARTAL JAZZ PIANO

BY PAUL RINZLER

To Joe Ryan, whose questions about jazz piano inspired this book.

ISBN 978-0-634-03573-9

HAL•LEONARD®
CORPORATION

7777 W. BLUEMOUND RD. P.O. BOX 13819 MILWAUKEE, WI 53213

Visit Hal Leonard Online at
www.halleonard.com

CONTENTS

Quartal jazz piano voicings are used very often by modern jazz pianists and have a special, captivating sound: they are open and clear but can be harmonically complex. The number of quartal voicings is large, so organizing and categorizing them can simplify learning and understanding them. This book was written in order to provide an easier approach to learning what could otherwise be a more complicated subject.

Recordings vs. theory

The voicings in this book were not created by collecting examples of voicings from jazz recordings, as is the approach in parts of some jazz piano books (for instance, Mark Levine's *Jazz Piano Book*, 1989, Sher Music Co.). Rather, they were created by including every possible quartal voicing that traditional jazz theory would allow. While any book may incorporate both approaches (Levine's book includes every possibility for some topics, and many of the voicings in this book can be found in many jazz recordings), each approach has its own strengths: a book that documents voicings taken from recordings is unquestionably authentic, while an approach that presents all theoretical possibilities may include creative options not previously considered.

How to use this book

The voicings in this book are presented in three sections: *All Voicings*, *Selected Voicings*, and *Quickest Voicings*. The most important difference between the sections is that they get progressively more restrictive: *All Voicings* contain every possible voicing according to the principles of jazz theory as well as some other limitations and possibilities (see "General Principles" and "Deriving the Voicings" for more information); *Selected Voicings* take all of the voicings from *All Voicings* but remove some, and *Quickest Voicings* take all of the voicings from *Selected Voicings* and remove yet more voicings. The same voicing may occur in all three sections or in two of them.

These sections differ with regard to:

> number of voicings
>
> number of keys
>
> number of notes doubled
>
> whether II-V-Is are complete
>
> whether 6-, 5-, and 4-note voicings are grouped together
>
> whether voicings included in other voicings with more notes ("Embedded voicings," see page 4) are shown separately
>
> visual layout

See "Overview" on page 8 for an overview of each section.

Most readers will primarily use each section in the following ways:

Quickest Voicings (pages 9-13)   the first and best quartal voicings one should know

Selected Voicings (pages 15-63)   a larger group of good quartal voicings in all keys

All Voicings (pages 65-69)   a complete presentation of all quartal voicings

Perfect fourths and other intervals

While the word "quartal" is used in this book to refer to voicings with all perfect fourths (P4ths) between adjacent notes in the voicing, some voicings that are not fully quartal (with non-P4th intervals) are included. For instance, the most common left hand voicings in jazz contain some voicings with all P4ths, but some with other intervals as well. In nearly every case only one interval in these voicings is not a P4th, and that interval is either a tritone or a major 3rd, both of which are only a half step away from a P4th. These left hand voicings are included in this book because (1) they are fundamental voicings, (2) they can easily support P4th right hand voicings, (3) they help make complete II-V-I progressions that do contain other voicings with all P4ths, and (4) having voicings for all chords in the II-V-I progression is important, given the significance of the II-V-I progression in jazz. Similarly, the So What voicing (a major 3rd on top of 3 P4ths) and is included in this book because (1) it is so common, (2) it contains all P4ths except for one major 3rd, and (3) it is very similar in sound to voicings with all P4ths. See "Deriving the Voicings," pp. 72-89 for complete information on how the voicings presented here were developed.

3 notes per hand

Because a quartal voicing that contains more than 3 notes is difficult to play with one hand, the voicings in this book are limited to 6 notes, 3 notes per hand. The right hand usually has the option of playing fewer than 3 notes, creating 4- and 5-note voicings.

Embedded voicings

"Embedded voicings" in this book refers to voicings that are contained within another voicing with more notes. For instance, any 5-note voicing with all P4ths contains a 4-note voicing with all P4ths:

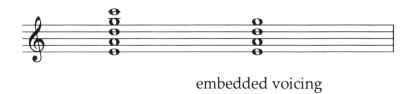

embedded voicing

The smaller voicing that is contained within the larger voicing is the embedded voicing. It is useful to distinguish embedded voicings because one can easily learn them by first learning the larger voicing they are contained within and then omitting notes. Embedded voicings are not shown in the *All Voicings* section and the *Selected Voicings* section, but are shown in the *Quickest Voicings* section, indicated by light shading around the embedded voicing.

Abbreviations and definitions

LH	left hand
RH	right hand
P4th	perfect fourth
quartal	all P4ths
m7	minor seventh chord
ø7	half-diminished seventh chord
7	dominant seventh chord
Δ7	major seventh chord (see the Appendix, pp. 90-91, for a complete outline of how to label chords)
extension	9th, 11th, or 13th of a chord, including chromatic alterations
II-V-I	This is a generic indication for either a IIm7 - V7 - IΔ7 (major key) or a IIø7 - V7 - Im7 (minor key) progression, including other variations for extensions if added and for other minor I chords, such as Im6, Im(Δ7), etc. It does not mean that all three chords are major triads, as upper case roman numerals sometimes imply.

GENERAL PRINCIPLES

The following is a brief outline of the principles on which the voicings in this book were generated. For complete information on how the voicings were generated, see "Deriving the Voicings," pages 72-89.

Quartal voicings use P4ths

- Only P4ths may occur between adjacent chord tones, with certain exceptions.

- Chords contain no more than 6 notes (the most 4ths easily played with both hands).

Voicings should be usable with the II-V-I progression

- The II-V-I is the most common progression in jazz.

- Any voicing part of the II-V- I progression can be used by itself when not part of a II-V-I progression.

Left hand voicings

Standard LH II-V-I voicings (A/B voicings) - page 72

- A/B voicings are the most common LH voicings.

- Some A/B voicings are not fully quartal but are included because they are nearly so and because they generate voicings necessary to complete some II-V-I progressions with fully quartal voicings.

- Extensions in A/B voicings may be chromatically altered in order to include all possible extensions.

- Variations on two fully quartal I chord voicings that substitute a nearby note for the 13th in the I chord are included because they are very common variations.

Other quartal voicings - page 73

- Other fully quartal voicings that are not A/B voicings are included.

Minor keys - pages 73-74

- Various alterations to major key II and I voicings are necessary to generate analogous voicings for minor keys because the qualities of the II and I chords are different in major and minor keys.

So What voicings - pages 75-76

- So What voicings contain all P4ths except for a major 3rd between the two upper notes.

- While So What voicings are not completely quartal, they are included in this book because (1) they are nearly so, (2) they are very common, and (3) they sound very much like true quartal voicings.

- Variations to the So What chord are necessary in order to generate analogous voicings with 4 and 6 notes and for minor keys.

RH voicings - pages 77-89

- All possible single notes, P4th intervals, and fully quartal 3-note voicings are potential RH voicings and may accompany any LH voicing.

Excluded RH voicings - RH voicings are excluded that contain

  - notes incompatible with chord tones or permissible extensions

  - a single RH note, and that note is not a P4th above the highest LH note (in order to make the single RH note quartal in some sense)

  - conflicting extensions
V chords	♭9 & 9, 9 & ♯9, 13 & ♭13
minor key II chords	♭9 & 9
minor key I chords	Δ7 & m7

  - notes a m2nd (or m9th) above a LH note (and the RH note is not doubled in the LH)

≤ Whole step between adjacent LH or RH II-V-I voicings

- Ideally, the lowest note of a LH or RH voicing should be no more than a whole step away from the lowest note of the next or previous LH or RH voicing in the II-V-I progression. This ensures a smooth connection between the chords in the progression.

- Some RH voicings exceed this guideline (as does one LH voicing) in order to make voicings for complete II-V-I progressions.

Enharmonic notation used

- Accidentals are used for convenience, without regard for enharmonic forms.

OVERVIEW

Voicings Section	Quickest pages 9-13	Selected pages 15-63	All pages 65-69
Number of voicings	54 (not including embedded voicings, see below)	106 (one key only)	163
Keys	CM, Cm	All	CM, Cm
II-V-Is	Complete	Some complete	Complete
6-, 5-, 4-note voicings	Grouped in separate sections	Grouped together	
Embedded voicings	Shown as separate voicings	Not shown as separate voicings	
	(An embedded voicing is a voicing that is part of another voicing that has more notes.)		
Included voicings	All from *Selected Voicings*	All from *All Voicings*	All LH voicings (pp. 72-74) All RH single notes, P4th intervals, quartal chords, and So What voicings

Excluded voicings	Voicings with any doublings (unless necessary to make a complete II-V-I)
	
	II chords in major with a 13th (B with Dm7)
	
	4-note voicings in which the RH note is not a P4th above highest LH note (So What variant OK).
		Voicings with any doublings (except 6-note voicings with 1 doubled note, which are included)	Voicings with:
			  incompatible extensions
			  notes incompatible with scale
			  single RH notes not P4th above highest LH note (except So What variation)
			  Δ7 with m7 in minor I chord
			  m2nd/m9th between notes in LH & RH (only if RH note is not doubled in LH)

Layout	LH & RH on grand staff; Voicings with same (or nearby) lowest RH note at same vertical position		RH: voicings with same lowest note on same staff LH: treble & bass clef voicings on separate pages

Summary

Number of voicings	54 (not including embedded voicings)
Keys	CM & Cm
II-V-Is	Complete
6-, 5-, 4-notes	Grouped in separate sections
Embedded voicings	Shown as separate voicings (An embedded voicing is a voicing that is part of another voicing that has more notes.)
Included voicings	All from *Selected Voicings*
Excluded voicings	Voicings with any doublings (unless necessary to make a complete II-V-I) II chords in major with a 13th (B with Dm7) 4-note voicings in which the RH note is not a P4th above highest LH note (So What variant OK).
Layout	LH & RH on grand staff Voicings with same (or nearby) lowest RH note at same vertical position

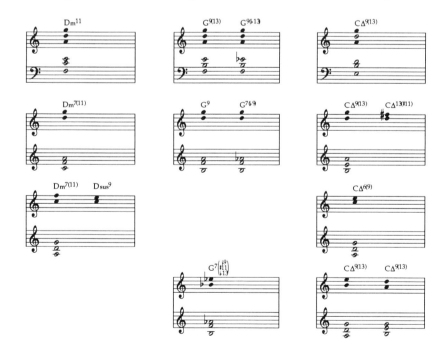

6-note voicings

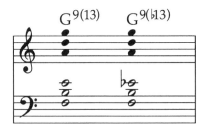
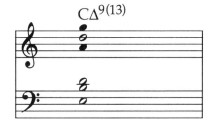

5-note voicings

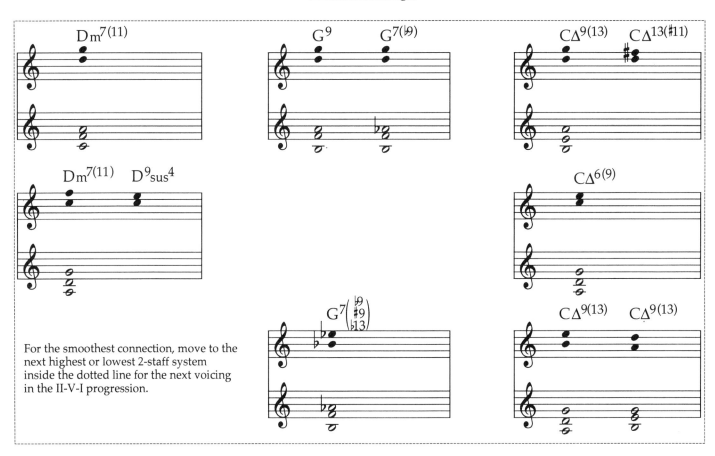

For the smoothest connection, move to the next highest or lowest 2-staff system inside the dotted line for the next voicing in the II-V-I progression.

● = RH note not doubled in LH

x = RH note doubled in LH at same octave

𝒐 = LH note; RH note doubled in LH

⬚ = part of another voicing that has more notes

4-note voicings

Quickest voicings

● = RH note not doubled in LH
x = RH note doubled in LH at same octave

○ = LH note; RH note doubled in LH
▢ = part of another voicing that has more notes

6-note voicings

5-note voicings

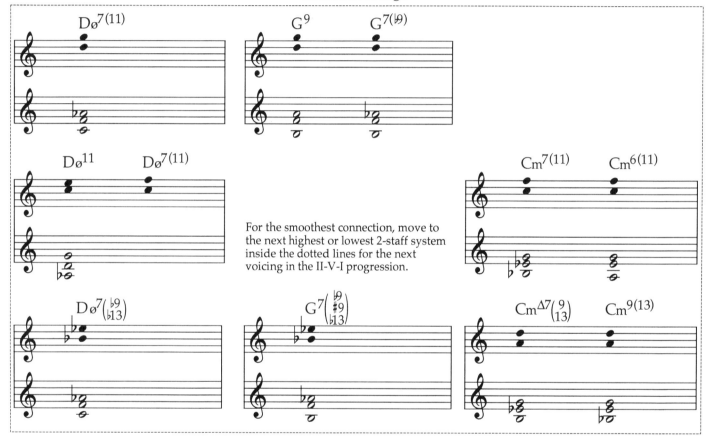

For the smoothest connection, move to the next highest or lowest 2-staff system inside the dotted lines for the next voicing in the II-V-I progression.

● = RH note not doubled in LH
x = RH note doubled in LH at same octave

𝒐 = LH note; RH note doubled in LH
☐ = part of another voicing that has more notes

4-note voicings

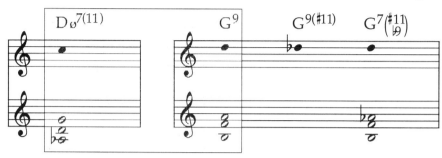

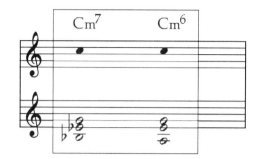

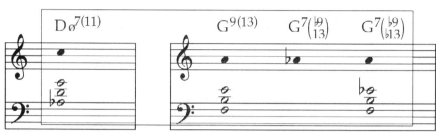

Summary

Number of voicings	106
Keys	All
II-V-Is	Some complete
6-, 5-, 4-notes	Grouped together
Embedded voicings	Not shown as separate voicings (An embedded voicing is a voicing that is part of another voicing that has more notes.)
Included voicings	All voicings from *All voicings*
Excluded voicings	Voicings with any doublings (except 6-note voicings with 1 doubled note, which are included)
Layout	LH & RH on grand staff
	Voicings with same (or nearby) lowest RH note on same vertical level

Selected voicings

For smoothest connection, move to next highest or lowest 2-staff system for the next voicing in the II-V-I progression.

● = RH note not doubled in LH   ○ = LH note; RH note doubled in LH   x = RH note doubled in LH at same octave

For smoothest connection, move to next highest or lowest 2-staff system for the next voicing in the II-V-I progression.

● = RH note not doubled in LH   ○ = LH note; RH note doubled in LH   x = RH note doubled in LH at same octave

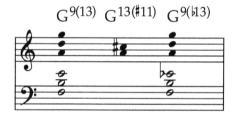

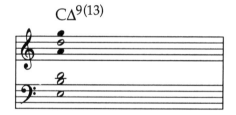

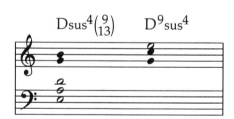

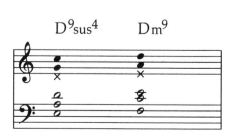

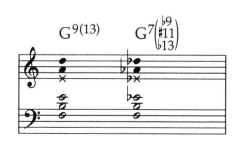

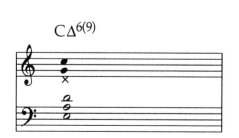

Selected voicings

For smoothest connection, move to next highest or lowest 2-staff system for the next voicing in the II-V-I progression.

● = RH note not doubled in LH   ○ = LH note; RH note doubled in LH   x = RH note doubled in LH at same octave

Selected voicings

For smoothest connection, move to next highest or lowest 2-staff system for the next voicing in the II-V-I progression.

● = RH note not doubled in LH   ○ = LH note; RH note doubled in LH   x = RH note doubled in LH at same octave

Selected voicings

For smoothest connection, move to next highest or lowest 2-staff system for the next voicing in the II-V-I progression.

● = RH note not doubled in LH   ○ = LH note; RH note doubled in LH   x = RH note doubled in LH at same octave

Selected voicings

For smoothest connection, move to next highest or lowest 2-staff system for the next voicing in the II-V-I progression.

● = RH note not doubled in LH   ○ = LH note; RH note doubled in LH   x = RH note doubled in LH at same octave

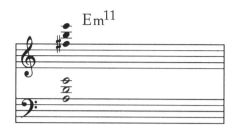

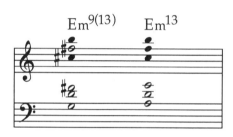

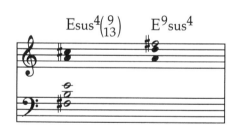

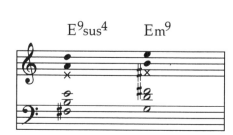

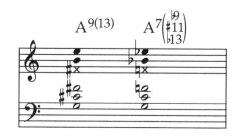

Selected voicings

For smoothest connection, move to next highest or lowest 2-staff system for the next voicing in the II-V-I progression.
● = RH note not doubled in LH   ○ = LH note; RH note doubled in LH   x = RH note doubled in LH at same octave

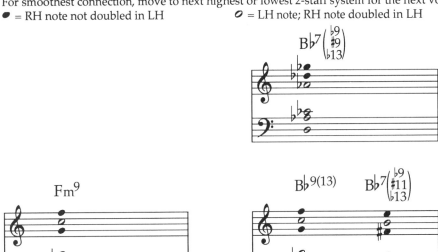

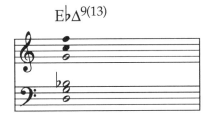

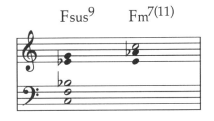

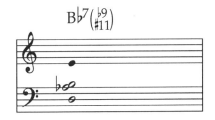

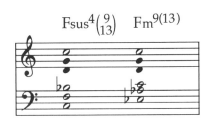

Selected voicings

For smoothest connection, move to next highest or lowest 2-staff system for the next voicing in the II-V-I progression.

● = RH note not doubled in LH   ◐ = LH note; RH note doubled in LH   x = RH note doubled in LH at same octave

Selected voicings

For smoothest connection, move to next highest or lowest 2-staff system for the next voicing in the II-V-I progression.

● = RH note not doubled in LH   ○ = LH note; RH note doubled in LH   x = RH note doubled in LH at same octave

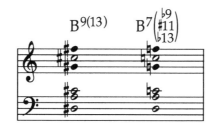

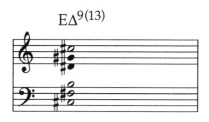

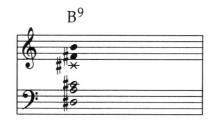
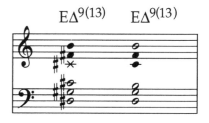

For smoothest connection, move to next highest or lowest 2-staff system for the next voicing in the II-V-I progression.

● = RH note not doubled in LH   𝑂 = LH note; RH note doubled in LH   x = RH note doubled in LH at same octave

Selected voicings

For smoothest connection, move to next highest or lowest 2-staff system for the next voicing in the II-V-I progression.

● = RH note not doubled in LH   ○ = LH note; RH note doubled in LH   x = RH note doubled in LH at same octave

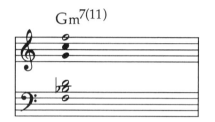

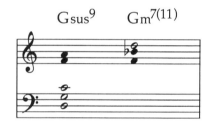

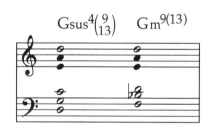

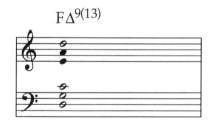

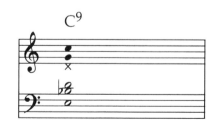
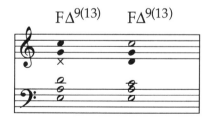

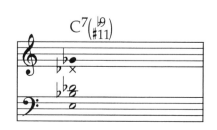
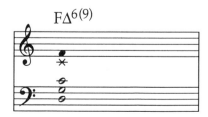

For smoothest connection, move to next highest or lowest 2-staff system for the next voicing in the II-V-I progression.
● = RH note not doubled in LH　　　　𝒐 = LH note; RH note doubled in LH　　　　x = RH note doubled in LH at same octave

Selected voicings

For smoothest connection, move to next highest or lowest 2-staff system for the next voicing in the II-V-I progression.

♩ = RH note not doubled in LH   o = LH note; RH note doubled in LH   x = RH note doubled in LH at same octave

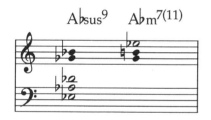

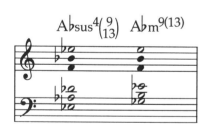

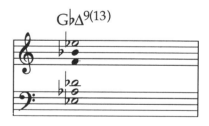

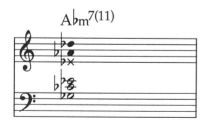

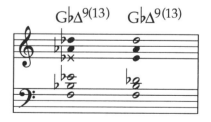

Selected voicings

For smoothest connection, move to next highest or lowest 2-staff system for the next voicing in the II-V-I progression.

● = RH note not doubled in LH   𝒐 = LH note; RH note doubled in LH   x = RH note doubled in LH at same octave

Selected voicings

For smoothest connection, move to next highest or lowest 2-staff system for the next voicing in the II-V-I progression.

● = RH note not doubled in LH   ○ = LH note; RH note doubled in LH   x = RH note doubled in LH at same octave

Selected voicings

For smoothest connection, move to next highest or lowest 2-staff system for the next voicing in the II-V-I progression.

● = RH note not doubled in LH   ◐ = LH note; RH note doubled in LH   x = RH note doubled in LH at same octave

Selected voicings

For smoothest connection, move to next highest or lowest 2-staff system for the next voicing in the II-V-I progression.

● = RH note not doubled in LH　　　　○ = LH note; RH note doubled in LH　　　　x = RH note doubled in LH at same octave

Selected voicings

For smoothest connection, move to next highest or lowest 2-staff system for the next voicing in the II-V-I progression.
● = RH note not doubled in LH   ○ = LH note; RH note doubled in LH   x = RH note doubled in LH at same octave

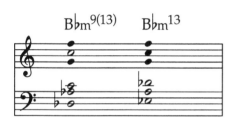

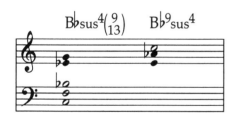

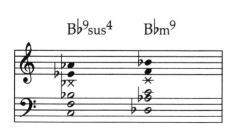

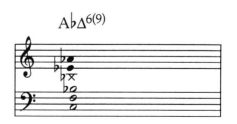

Selected voicings

For smoothest connection, move to next highest or lowest 2-staff system for the next voicing in the II-V-I progression.

● = RH note not doubled in LH   ○ = LH note; RH note doubled in LH   x = RH note doubled in LH at same octave

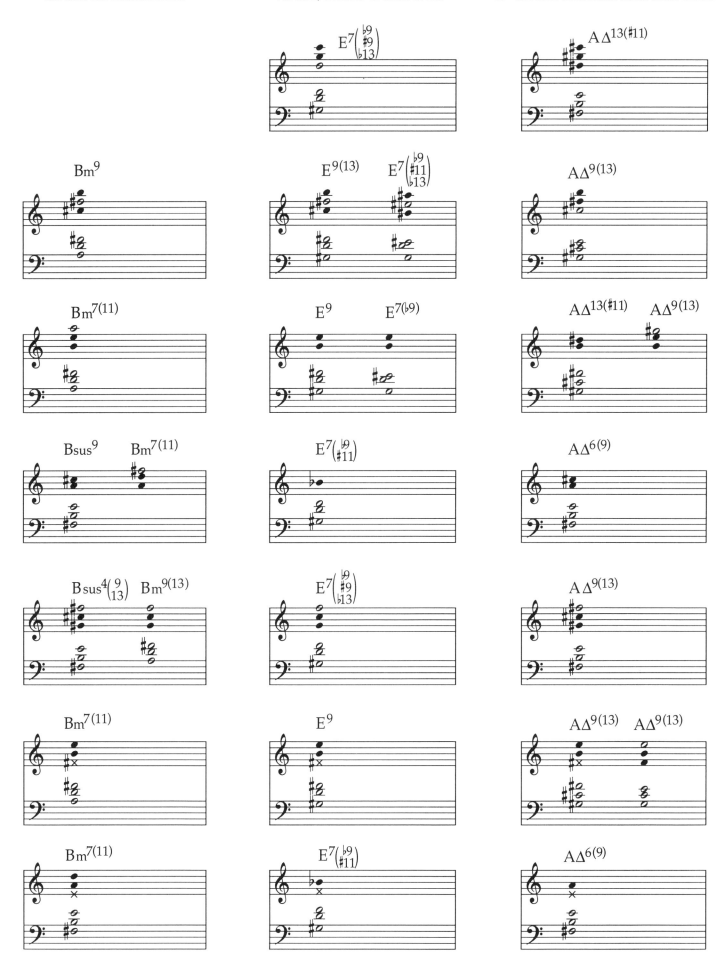

For smoothest connection, move to next highest or lowest 2-staff system for the next voicing in the II-V-I progression.

● = RH note not doubled in LH   ○ = LH note; RH note doubled in LH   x = RH note doubled in LH at same octave

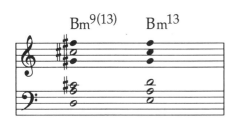

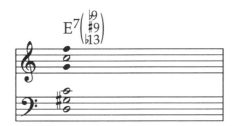

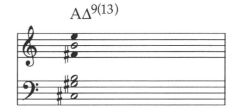

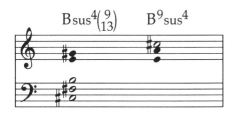

Selected voicings

For smoothest connection, move to next highest or lowest 2-staff system for the next voicing in the II-V-I progression.

● = RH note not doubled in LH   ○ = LH note; RH note doubled in LH   x = RH note doubled in LH at same octave

For smoothest connection, move to next highest or lowest 2-staff system for the next voicing in the II-V-I progression.

● = RH note not doubled in LH   𝒐 = LH note; RH note doubled in LH   x = RH note doubled in LH at same octave

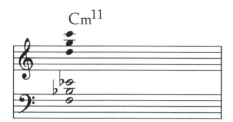

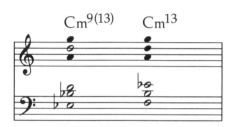

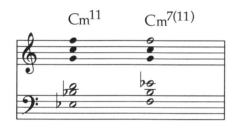

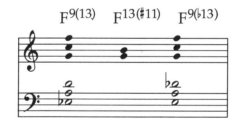

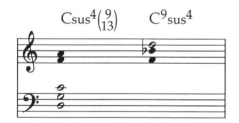

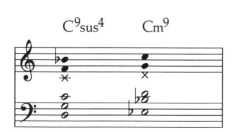

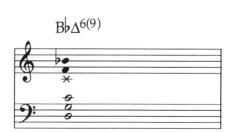

Selected voicings

For smoothest connection, move to next highest or lowest 2-staff system for the next voicing in the II-V-I progression.

● = RH note not doubled in LH   ○ = LH note; RH note doubled in LH   x = RH note doubled in LH at same octave

Selected voicings

For smoothest connection, move to next highest or lowest 2-staff system for the next voicing in the II-V-I progression.

● = RH note not doubled in LH   o = LH note; RH note doubled in LH   x = RH note doubled in LH at same octave

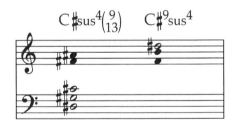

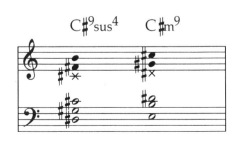

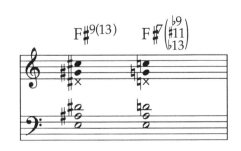

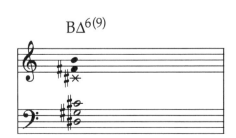

Selected voicings

For smoothest connection, move to next highest or lowest 2-staff system for the next voicing in the II-V-I progression.

● = RH note not doubled in LH   ○ = LH note; RH note doubled in LH   x = RH note doubled in LH at same octave

For smoothest connection, move to next highest or lowest 2-staff system for the next voicing in the II-V-I progression.

● = RH note not doubled in LH   ○ = LH note; RH note doubled in LH   x = RH note doubled in LH at same octave

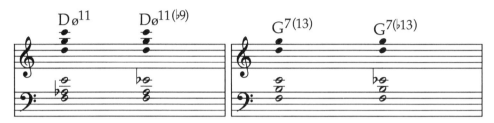

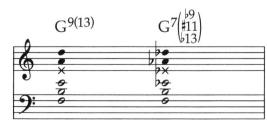

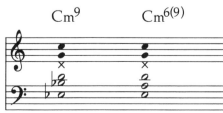

Selected voicings

For smoothest connection, move to next highest or lowest 2-staff system for the next voicing in the II-V-I progression.

● = RH note not doubled in LH   ○ = LH note; RH note doubled in LH   x = RH note doubled in LH at same octave

For smoothest connection, move to next highest or lowest 2-staff system for the next voicing in the II-V-I progression.
● = RH note not doubled in LH   ○ = LH note; RH note doubled in LH   x = RH note doubled in LH at same octave

Selected voicings

For smoothest connection, move to next highest or lowest 2-staff system for the next voicing in the II-V-I progression.

● = RH note not doubled in LH   𝅗𝅥 = LH note; RH note doubled in LH   x = RH note doubled in LH at same octave

For smoothest connection, move to next highest or lowest 2-staff system for the next voicing in the II-V-I progression.

● = RH note not doubled in LH   ○ = LH note; RH note doubled in LH   x = RH note doubled in LH at same octave

Selected voicings

For smoothest connection, move to next highest or lowest 2-staff system for the next voicing in the II-V-I progression.

● = RH note not doubled in LH　　　　　　　𝐨 = LH note; RH note doubled in LH　　　　　　　x = RH note doubled in LH at same octave

For smoothest connection, move to next highest or lowest 2-staff system for the next voicing in the II-V-I progression.

♥ = RH note not doubled in LH   ○ = LH note; RH note doubled in LH   x = RH note doubled in LH at same octave

Selected voicings

For smoothest connection, move to next highest or lowest 2-staff system for the next voicing in the II-V-I progression.

● = RH note not doubled in LH   𝒐 = LH note; RH note doubled in LH   x = RH note doubled in LH at same octave

For smoothest connection, move to next highest or lowest 2-staff system for the next voicing in the II-V-I progression.
● = RH note not doubled in LH   𝆲 = LH note; RH note doubled in LH   x = RH note doubled in LH at same octave

Selected voicings

For smoothest connection, move to next highest or lowest 2-staff system for the next voicing in the II-V-I progression.

● = RH note not doubled in LH   ○ = LH note; RH note doubled in LH   x = RH note doubled in LH at same octave

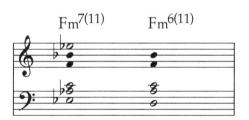

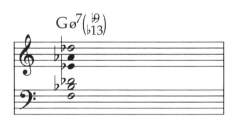

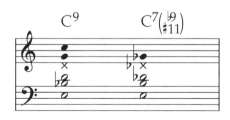

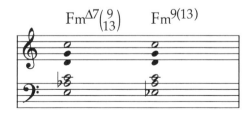

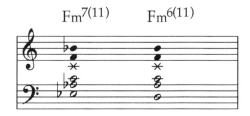

For smoothest connection, move to next highest or lowest 2-staff system for the next voicing in the II-V-I progression.

● = RH note not doubled in LH   ○ = LH note; RH note doubled in LH   x = RH note doubled in LH at same octave

Selected voicings

For smoothest connection, move to next highest or lowest 2-staff system for the next voicing in the II-V-I progression.
● = RH note not doubled in LH   𝑶 = LH note; RH note doubled in LH   x = RH note doubled in LH at same octave

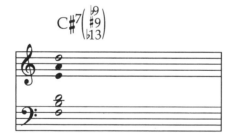

For smoothest connection, move to next highest or lowest 2-staff system for the next voicing in the II-V-I progression.

● = RH note not doubled in LH   ○ = LH note; RH note doubled in LH   x = RH note doubled in LH at same octave

Selected voicings

For smoothest connection, move to next highest or lowest 2-staff system for the next voicing in the II-V-I progression.

● = RH note not doubled in LH   ⊘ = LH note; RH note doubled in LH   x = RH note doubled in LH at same octave

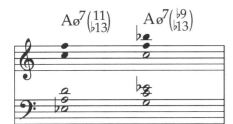

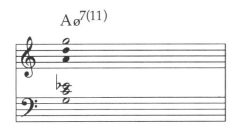

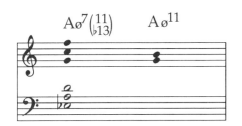

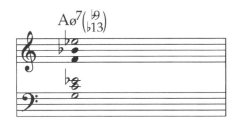

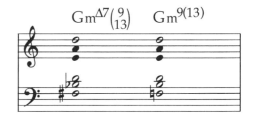

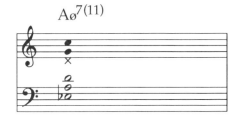

For smoothest connection, move to next highest or lowest 2-staff system for the next voicing in the II-V-I progression.

● = RH note not doubled in LH   ○ = LH note; RH note doubled in LH   x = RH note doubled in LH at same octave

Selected voicings

For smoothest connection, move to next highest or lowest 2-staff system for the next voicing in the II-V-I progression.

● = RH note not doubled in LH   ○ = LH note; RH note doubled in LH   x = RH note doubled in LH at same octave

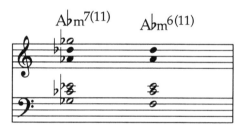

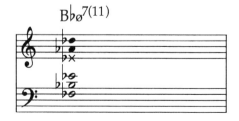

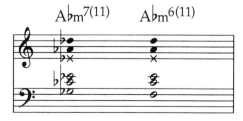

For smoothest connection, move to next highest or lowest 2-staff system for the next voicing in the II-V-I progression.

● = RH note not doubled in LH   ○ = LH note; RH note doubled in LH   x = RH note doubled in LH at same octave

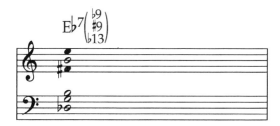

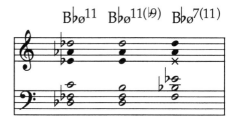

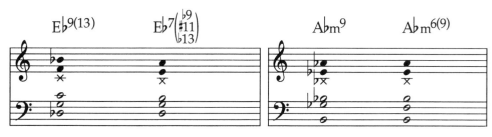

Selected voicings

For smoothest connection, move to next highest or lowest 2-staff system for the next voicing in the II-V-I progression.

● = RH note not doubled in LH   ○ = LH note; RH note doubled in LH   x = RH note doubled in LH at same octave

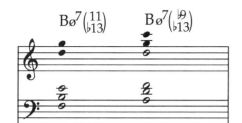

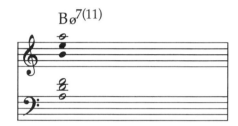

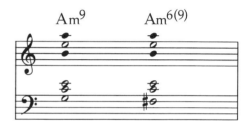

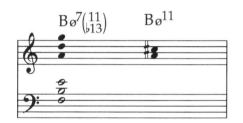

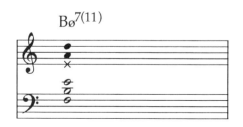

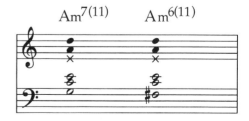

For smoothest connection, move to next highest or lowest 2-staff system for the next voicing in the II-V-I progression.

● = RH note not doubled in LH   ○ = LH note; RH note doubled in LH   x = RH note doubled in LH at same octave

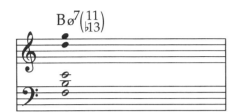

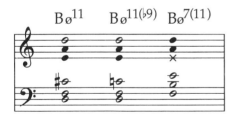

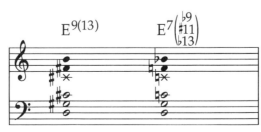

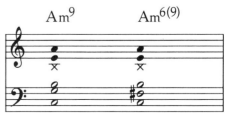

Selected voicings

For smoothest connection, move to next highest or lowest 2-staff system for the next voicing in the II-V-I progression.

● = RH note not doubled in LH   ○ = LH note; RH note doubled in LH   x = RH note doubled in LH at same octave

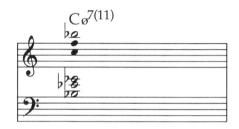

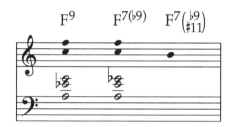

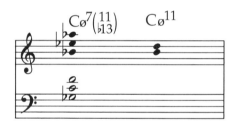

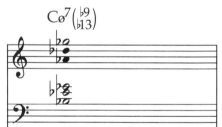

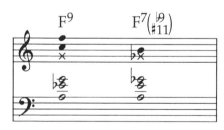

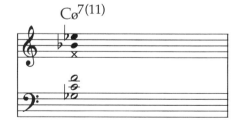

For smoothest connection, move to next highest or lowest 2-staff system for the next voicing in the II-V-I progression.
● = RH note not doubled in LH   ◐ = LH note; RH note doubled in LH   x = RH note doubled in LH at same octave

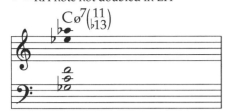

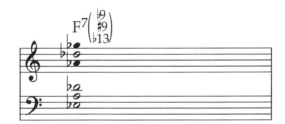

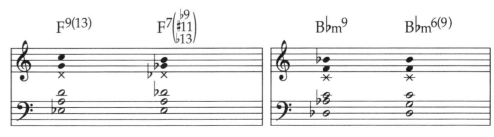

Selected voicings

For smoothest connection, move to next highest or lowest 2-staff system for the next voicing in the II-V-I progression.

● = RH note not doubled in LH   ○ = LH note; RH note doubled in LH   x = RH note doubled in LH at same octave

For smoothest connection, move to next highest or lowest 2-staff system for the next voicing in the II-V-I progression.

● = RH note not doubled in LH   ○ = LH note; RH note doubled in LH   x = RH note doubled in LH at same octave

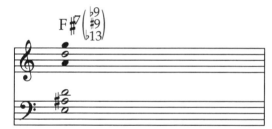

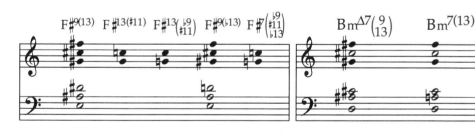

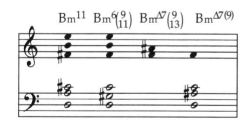

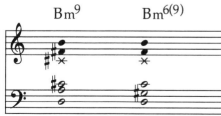

Summary

Number of voicings	163
Keys	CM & Cm
II-V-Is	Complete
6-, 5-, 4-notes	Grouped together
Embedded voicings	Not shown (An embedded voicing is a voicing that is part of another voicing that has more notes.)
Included voicings	All LH voicings (pp. 72-74)
	All RH single notes, P4th intervals, quartal chords, and So What voicings (pp. 75-89)
Excluded voicings	Voicings with

incompatible extensions
notes incompatible with scale
single RH notes not P4th above highest LH note (except So
    What variation)
Δ7 with m7 in minor I chord
˙m2nd/m9th between notes in LH & RH (only if RH note
    not doubled in LH)

Layout (RH)	Voicings with same lowest RH note on same staff
Layout (LH)	Treble & bass clef voicings on separate pages

● = RH note not doubled in LH   ○ = LH note; RH note doubled in LH   x = RH note doubled in LH at same octave

● = RH note not doubled in LH   ○ = LH note; RH note doubled in LH   x = RH note doubled in LH at same octave

Dm7 **G7** **CΔ7**

All voicings

● = RH note not doubled in LH   ○ = LH note; RH note doubled in LH   x = RH note doubled in LH at same octave

Dø7   G7   Cm

● = RH note not doubled in LH   ○ = LH note; RH note doubled in LH   x = RH note doubled in LH at same octave

VOICINGS FOR A JAZZ STANDARD

The following example shows one possible application of the quartal voicings in this book to the chord progression for a well-known jazz standard.

1. The same RH quartal chord (F - B♭ - E♭) can be used as part of a series of chords (in this case, 4 consecutive chords).

2. Adjacent voicings with different number of notes can be used.

3. Chromatically parallel RH quartal chords can be used for the II-V-I progression.

A.

B.

C.

DERIVING THE VOICINGS

LH Voicings

Standard LH A/B voicings[2]

Ⓐ voicings - 3rd of the chord is the lowest note

Ⓑ voicings - 7th of the chord is the lowest note

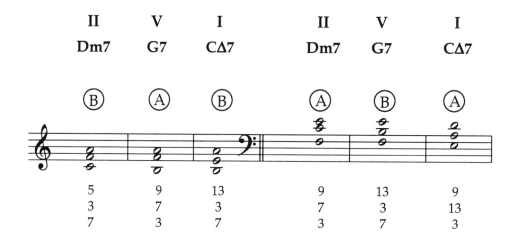

- A/B voicings alternate through the II-V-I progression (A-B-A or B-A-B).
- A and B I chord voicings are quartal.
- The V chord Ⓑ voicing is nearly quartal (contains a tritone and P4th).
- The range for all notes in the LH voicings (in any key) is an octave on either side of middle C.[3]

---

[2] Dan Haerle, *The Jazz Language* (Hialeah, Florida: Studio 224, 1980), 24; and Mark Levine, *The Jazz Piano Book* (Petaluma, CA: Sher Music Co., 1989), 46.

[3] Dan Haerle, *Jazz/Rock Voicings*, (Lebanon, Indiana: Studio P/R, 1974), iii. This range can be considered a maximum range; some voicings at the extremes of this range might need to be moved to another octave depending on individual choice.

Extra LH voicings

<u>Chord</u>   <u>Extra voicings</u>

II (Dm7)   • three quartal voicings no more than a M2nd away from V chord voicings

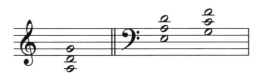

V (G7)   • two voicings with chromatically altered extensions (♭9 and ♭13)

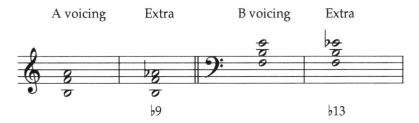

I (CΔ7)   • one voicing in which 5 substitutes for 13

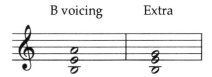

• one voicing in which 7 substitutes for 13

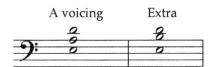

(While the above extra I chord voicings are not quartal, they are included because they are common variations on true quartal I chord voicings.)

• one quartal voicing no more than a M2nd away from a V chord voicing

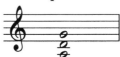

Minor keys

Modifications to the major key LH voicings for II and I chords are necessary for II and I chords in minor keys (V chord voicings remain the same in major or minor keys because the quality of the V chord—dominant 7th—remains the same for major and minor keys).

Deriving the voicings

II chord modifications

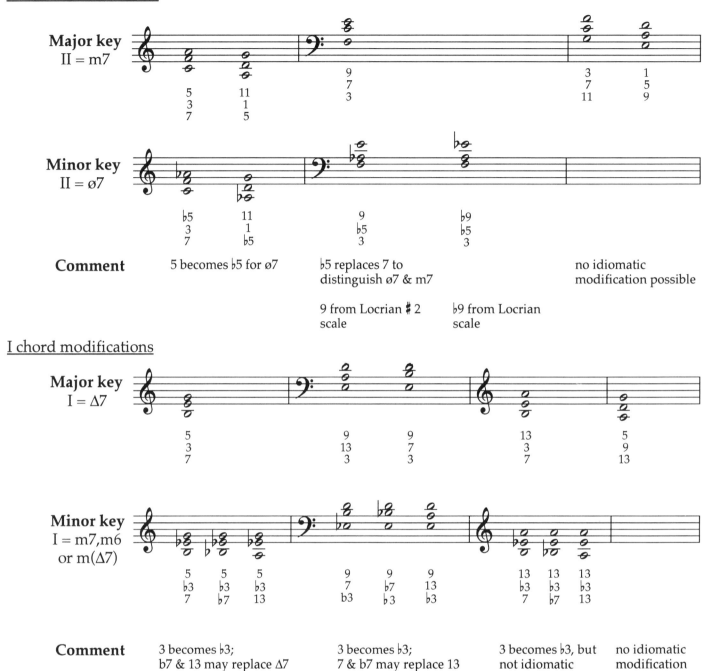

Major key
II = m7

5	11
3	1
7	5

9
7
3

3
7
11

1
5
9

Minor key
II = ø7

b5
3
7

11
1
b5

9
b5
3

b9
b5
3

Comment

5 becomes b5 for ø7

b5 replaces 7 to distinguish ø7 & m7

9 from Locrian ♯2 scale

b9 from Locrian scale

no idiomatic modification possible

I chord modifications

Major key
I = Δ7

5
3
7

9
13
3

9
7
3

13
3
7

5
9
13

Minor key
I = m7, m6
or m(Δ7)

5	5	5
b3	b3	b3
7	b7	13

9	9	9
7	b7	13
b3	b3	b3

13	13	13
b3	b3	b3
7	b7	13

Comment

3 becomes b3;
b7 & 13 may replace Δ7

3 becomes b3;
7 & b7 may replace 13

3 becomes b3, but not idiomatic

no idiomatic modification possible

Summary of LH minor key voicings

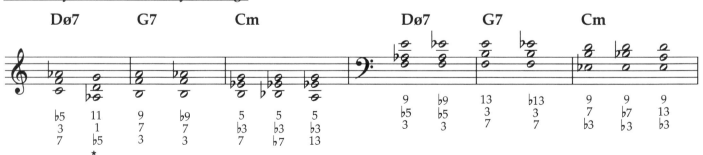

Dø7		G7		Cm		
b5	11	9	b9	5	5	5
3	1	7	7	b3	b3	b3
7	b5	3	3	7	b7	13

*

Dø7		G7		Cm		
9	b9	13	b13	9	9	9
b5	b5	3	3	7	b7	13
3	3	7	7	b3	b3	b3

* The one exception to the guideline that voicings may be no more than a M2nd away from the next voicing in the II-V-I progression is the 11-1-b5 voicing which moves 3 half-steps to either the A or B LH voicing (treble and bass clef above) for the V chord.

So What Chord

4- and 6-note variations

The So What chord is 3 P4ths and a M3rd on top. In order to have So What chords compatible with 4- and 6-note quartal chords, variations on the So What chord may be developed by adding or subtracting a P4th. The resulting chords still retain much of the sound of the So What chord because they still contain several P4ths with a M3rd on top.

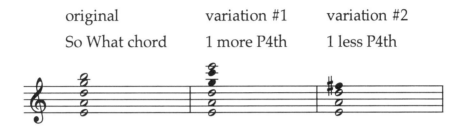

Minor key variations

Because no minor key LH voicing or LH V chord voicing is a true quartal chord, another variation in the So What chord is necessary in order to create So What voicings for minor keys. A single change to the So What chord—a tritone, not a P4th, as the lowest interval of the chord—can create minor key So What voicings. (The LH V chord So What voicing—a P4th and a tritone—will work for both minor keys and major keys.)

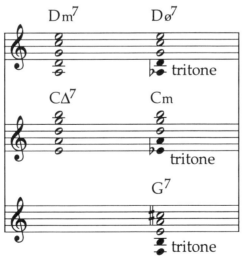

Deriving the voicings

<u>Summary of So What chord and variations</u>

Only quartal LH voicings or LH voicings with the tritone variation (page 75) can be used as part of a So What chord. The following shows the So What chord and its 4- and 6-note variations based on these LH voicings.

- ● = incompatible RH note (not an extension for the prevailing chord); voicings containing such notes are excluded

RH Voicings

RH quartal voicings

Quartal voicings for the RH may be produced by stacking two P4ths on each note of the chromatic scale.

Incompatible notes in RH voicings

Not all RH quartal voicings can be used with all chords in the II-V-I progression. Below are listed several principles by which RH quartal voicings will be omitted and which are reflected in Table 1, "Excluded notes in RH voicings" (pages 79-89).

The remaining voicings not excluded are included in the *All Voicings* section (pages 65-69).

Incompatible notes

RH voicings are excluded if they contain a note that is incompatible with the prevailing chord (that is, is not part of the chord or its traditional extensions). For reference, scales that contain all idiomatic chord tones and extensions are included for each chord in Table 1. (Not every scale used by an improviser needs to be included in order to show all possible chord tones and extensions.)

Single notes

Single RH notes are excluded if they are not a P4th above the highest LH note (in order to retain some connection to quartal harmony). The only exception is the 4-note variation of the So What chord in which the single RH note is a M3rd above the highest LH note. (All P4th intervals and 3-note quartal chords are included for the RH.)

Conflicting chord tones

A RH quartal voicing is excluded if it contains a note that
  • is a different chromatic version of the same extension in the LH:

  V chords:
      ♭9 & 9
      9 & #9 (♭9 & #9 is allowed)
      13 & ♭13
  II chords:
      ♭9 & 9

Deriving the voicings

- is the m7th of a minor key I chord that also contains the M7th (and vice versa), or
- forms a m9th or m2nd with a note in a LH voicing (and is not doubled in the LH).

These voicings are excluded to avoid harmonic conflicts. The m2nd/m9th is an uncharacteristic dissonance for quartal chords, and different versions of the same extension in most cases are not idiomatic.

So What chords

So What voicings are included in Table 1. Assuming the LH plays the lower 3 notes in every voicing, it is not necessary to list all chromatic RH components of So What chords: for any given LH voicing that can support a So What chord (quartal or tritone/P4th variation), there are only 3 RH So What voicings possible (one So What chord and two variations).

Excluding RH quartal voicings for a single incompatible note

By including all RH single notes, intervals, and 3-note chords, no possible voicing is missed by excluding a voicing even if only one of its notes are incompatible (because the note or notes not incompatible are included elsewhere as valid voicings).

Two or more incompatible notes

Some voicings may have two or three incompatible RH notes. Only one note is sometimes indicated in Table 1 as incompatible—usually a note not compatible with the prevailing scale—because only one note is sufficient to exclude a voicing.

Incompatible note doubled in the LH

Voicings with an incompatible note that is doubled in the LH are not excluded.

Table 1 - Excluded notes in RH Voicings

All RH quartal voicings—single notes, P4th intervals, 3-note quartal chords, and the RH component of the So What chord and its variations—are shown with every LH voicing to determine which RH voicings are incompatible with the LH voicing. Notes incompatible with the prevailing scale are the same for each chord regardless of the LH voicing, and so are duplicated for each LH voicing of the same chord in the three staves above the voicing.

Key

●	excluded RH note
7,9,13	voicing with conflicting chord tones or extensions
m9	voicing with m9th (or m2nd) interval
Ⓝ	voicing with single RH note not a P4th above highest LH note
s	voicing with note incompatible with prevailing scale(s)
SW	So What voicing or variation

C MAJOR

II chord - Dm7

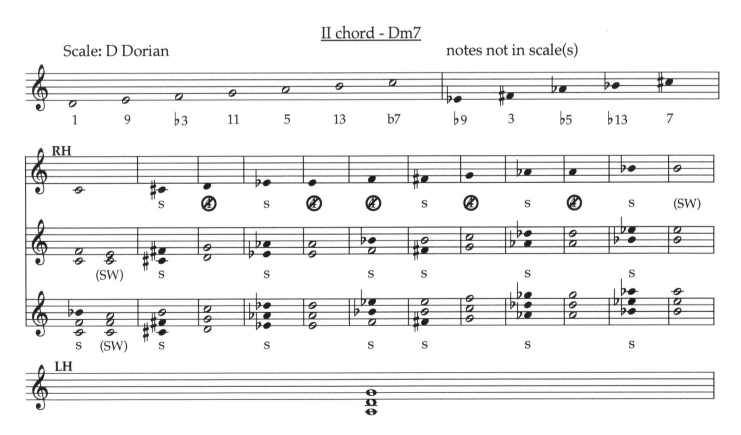

Deriving the voicings

Key
- ●   excluded RH note
- 7,9,13   voicing with conflicting chord tones or extensions
- m9   voicing with m9th (or m2nd) interval
- Ⓟ4   voicing with single RH note not a P4th above highest LH note
- s   voicing with note incompatible with prevailing scale(s)
- SW   So What voicing or variation

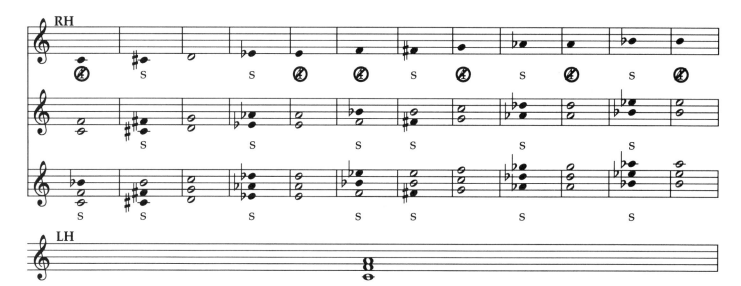

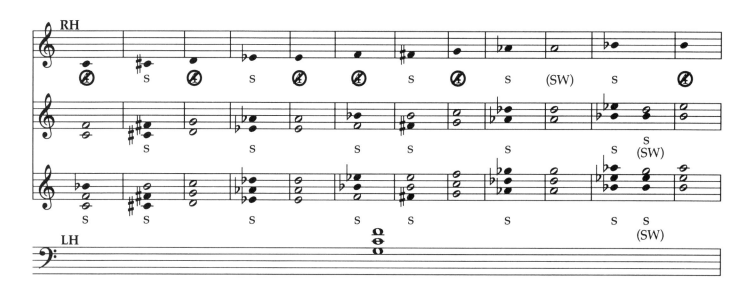

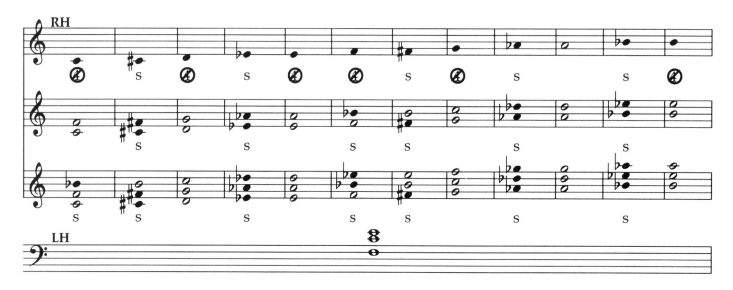

Key

●	excluded RH note
7,9,13	voicing with conflicting chord tones or extensions
m9	voicing with m9th (or m2nd) interval
⊘4	voicing with single RH note not a P4th above highest LH note
s	voicing with note incompatible with prevailing scale(s)
SW	So what voicing or variation

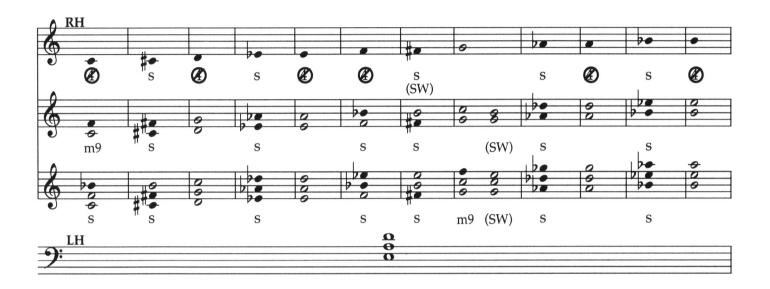

V chord - G7

Scale: G Mixoydian   notes not in scales

1	9	3	11	5	13	♭7	11	7

Scale: G Altered (diminished whole-tone)

1	♭9	♯9	3	♭5	♭13	♭7

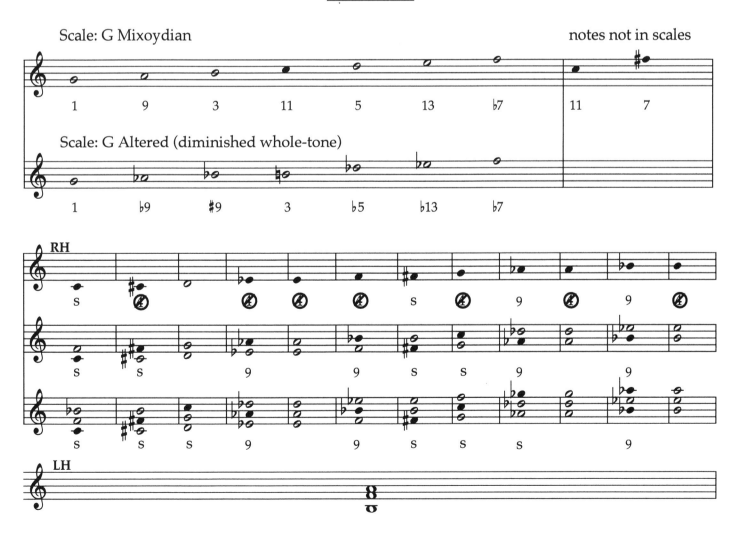

Deriving the voicings

Key

●	excluded RH note
7,9,13	voicing with conflicting chord tones or extensions
m9	voicing with m9th (or m2nd) interval
Ⓝ	voicing with single RH note not a P4th above highest LH note
s	voicing with note incompatible with prevailing scale(s)
SW	So What voicing or variation

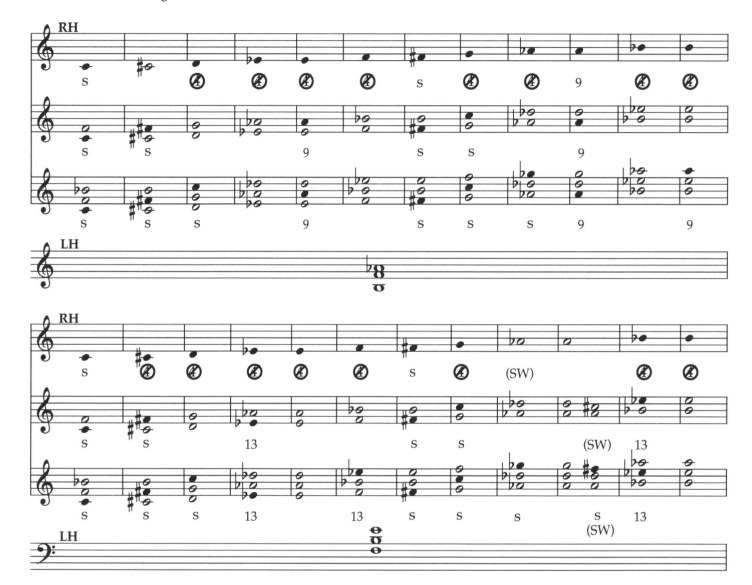

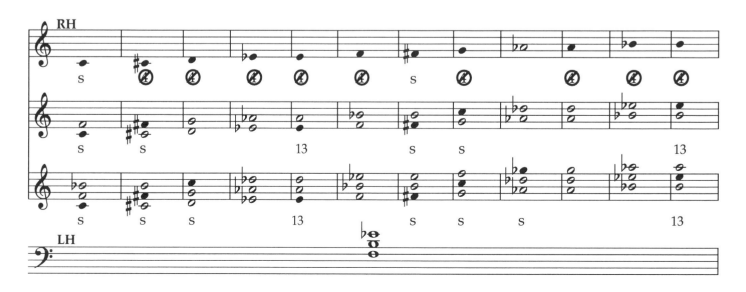

Key

●	excluded RH note
7,9,13	voicing with conflicting chord tones or extensions
m9	voicing with m9th (or m2nd) interval
ⓘ4	voicing with single RH note not a P4th above highest LH note
s	voicing with note incompatible with prevailing scale(s)
SW	So what voicing or variation

I chord - CΔ7

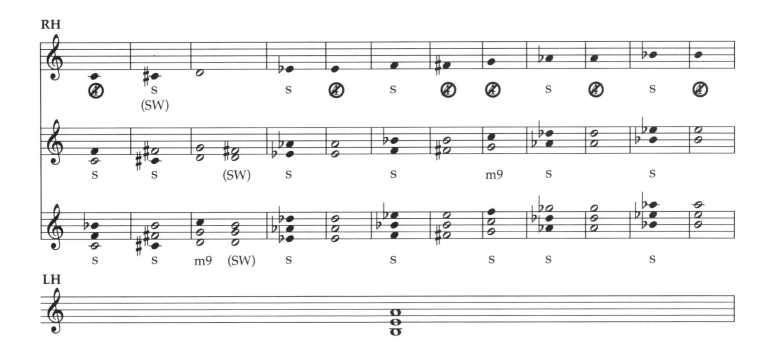

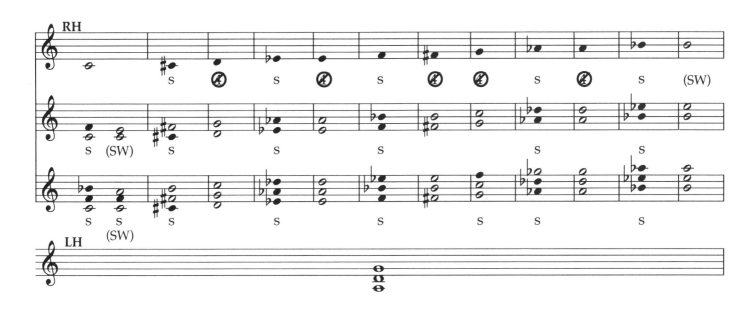

Deriving the voicings

Key

- ●   excluded RH note
- 7,9,13   voicing with conflicting chord tones or extensions
- m9   voicing with m9th (or m2nd) interval
- ✗   voicing with single RH note not a P4th above highest LH note
- s   voicing with note incompatible with prevailing scale(s)
- SW   So What voicing or variation

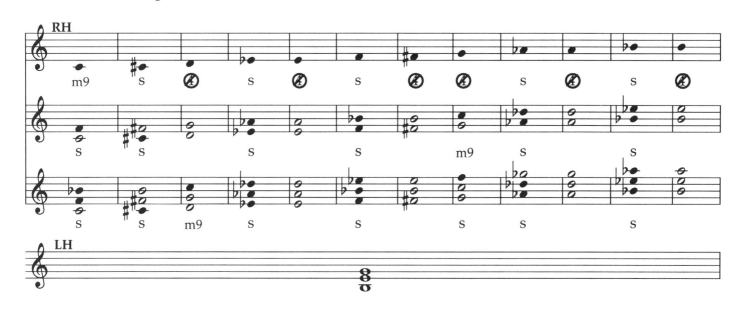

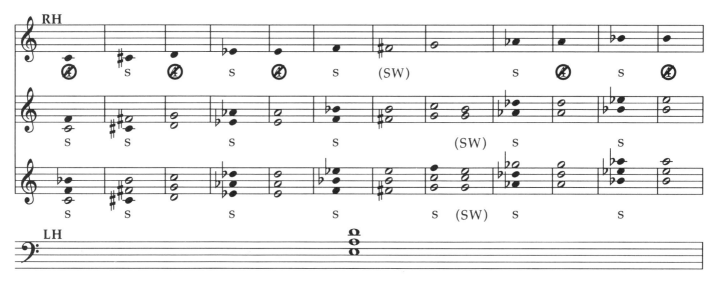

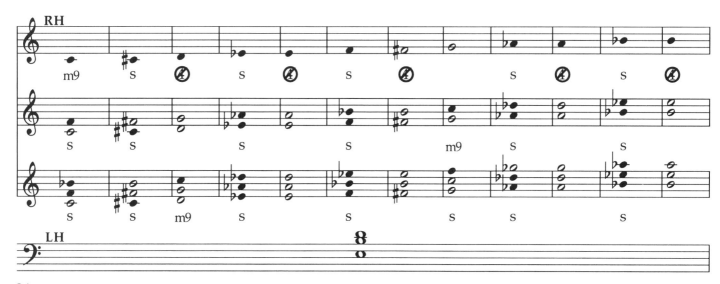

Key

- **♩**   excluded RH note
- **7, 9, 13**   voicing with conflicting chord tones or extensions
- **m9**   voicing with m9th interval
- **Ⓐ**   voicing with single RH note not a P4th above highest LH note
- **s**   voicing with note incompatible with prevailing scale(s)
- **SW**   So What voicing or variation

C MINOR

II chord (Dø7)

Deriving the voicings

Key
●	excluded RH note
7, 9, 13	voicing with conflicting chord tones or extensions
m9	voicing with m9th interval
Ⓐ	voicing with single RH note not a P4th above highest LH note
s	voicing with note incompatible with prevailing scale(s)
SW	So What voicing or variation

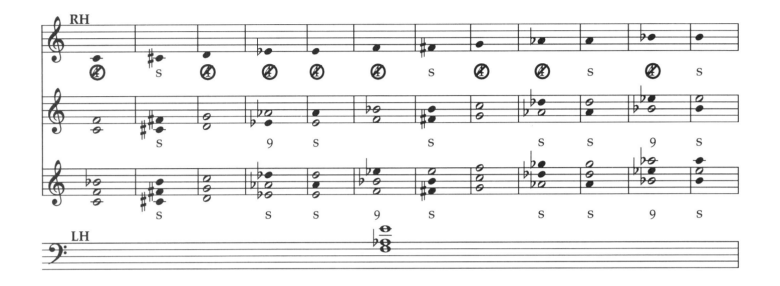

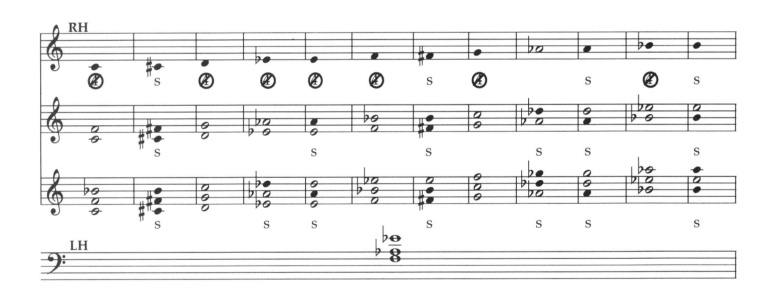

V chord - G7

(same as major key, see pp. 81-82)

Key

🕳	excluded RH note
7, 9, 13	voicing with conflicting chord tones or extensions
m9	voicing with m9th interval
Ⓝ	voicing with single RH note not a P4th above highest LH note
s	voicing with note incompatible with prevailing scale(s)
SW	So What voicing or variation

I chord - Cm6, Cm7, Cm (Δ7)

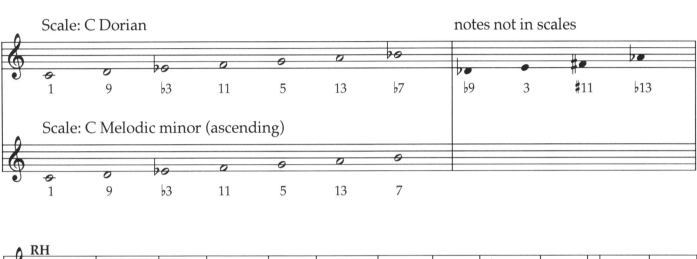

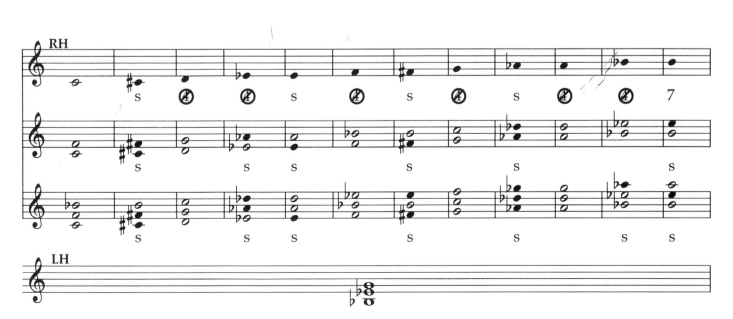

Deriving the voicings

Key

●	excluded RH note
7, 9, 13	voicing with conflicting chord tones or extensions
m9	voicing with m9th interval
ⓩ	voicing with single RH note not a P4th above highest LH note
s	voicing with note incompatible with prevailing scale(s)
SW	So What voicing or variation

Key

●	excluded RH note
7, 9, 13	voicing with conflicting chord tones or extensions
m9	voicing with m9th interval
Ⓐ	voicing with single RH note not a P4th above highest LH note
s	voicing with note incompatible with prevailing scale(s)
SW	So What voicing or variation

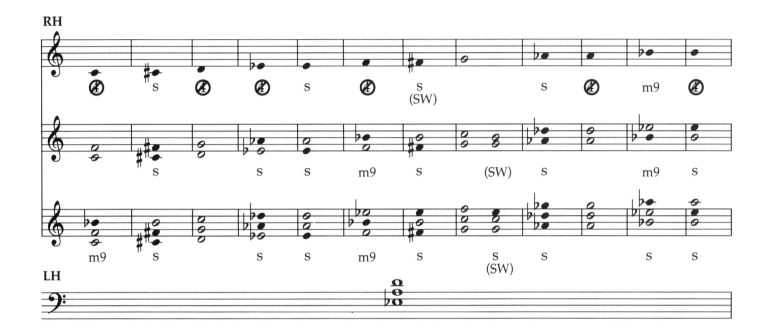

APPENDIX: Chord symbols

Principles	Examples
Chord symbols for jazz chords contain	
a letter, representing the root	C [or any letter representing a pitch]
a symbol, representing the quality	<table><tr><td><u>Symbol</u></td><td><u>Quality name</u></td></tr><tr><td>Δ or M or Maj</td><td>major</td></tr><tr><td>[blank]</td><td>dominant</td></tr><tr><td>m or - or min</td><td>minor</td></tr><tr><td>ø or m7(♭5)</td><td>half-diminished</td></tr><tr><td>o</td><td>diminished</td></tr><tr><td>mΔ7</td><td>minor major-7</td></tr></table>
a number	<table><tr><td><u>Number</u></td><td><u>Applicable qualities</u></td></tr><tr><td>7, 9, 11, 13</td><td>any</td></tr><tr><td>6</td><td>M, m, or ø</td></tr></table>
"sus4" may also follow a letter or a number.	
The sus2 chord is sometimes recognized.	
Basic jazz chords	
<u>A chord with a</u> <u>is labeled as a</u> 6th & no 7th 6th chord 6th & a 7th 7(13) chord	

The number immediately after the quality symbol means that all lower chord tones are present in the chord.	*(musical notation: Cm7, Cm9, Cm11)*
Extensions without all other chord tones below it are placed in parentheses.	*(musical notation: Cm7(11), Cm7(11/13))*
Extensions with chromatic alterations are placed in parentheses.	*(musical notation: C13(#11), C7(b9/#11/b13))*
For consistency, in this book a voicing with a ♭5 is labeled with a ♯11 (except for ø7 chords)	*(musical notation: C7(b9/#11))*
a voicing with no 3rd is labeled as if it had the appropriate 3rd (except for the sus4 chord)	*(musical notation: Dm(9))*
a ø7 voicing with no 7th is labeled as if it had the 7th	*(musical notation: Dø7(11/b13))*

INDEX OF VOICINGS

Voicings that appear in more than one section (voicings from *Quickest voicings* appear in *Selected voicings*, and voicings in *Selected voicings* appear in *All voicings*) are also duplicated below for every section in which they appear.

For *Selected voicings* in keys other than CM and Cm, find the voicing in the key of CM or Cm and go to the nearby corresponding page in the *Selected voicings* section for the voicing in other keys.

Chord	Group	Page number	# of voicings
Dm(9)	All	67	1
Dm6(9)	All	67	1
Dm7	Quickest	11	1
	All	66	1
Dm7(11)	Quickest	10	3
		11	1
	Selected	16	4
		17	1
	All	66	5
		67	4
Dm9	Quickest	10	1
		11	1
	Selected	16	1
		17	1
	All	66	1
		67	2
Dm9(13)	Selected	16	1
		17	1
	All	66	1
		67	1
Dm11	Quickest	10	1
	Selected	17	3
	All	67	4
Dm13	Selected	17	1
	All	67	1
Dsus4	All	66	1
Dsus4(9)	Quickest	11	1
	All	66	1
		67	1
Dsus4(9,13)	Selected	16	1
		17	1
	All	66	1
		67	1
D7sus4	Quickest	11	1
	All	66	1
D9sus4	Quickest	10	2
	Selected	16	1
		17	2
	All	66	1
		67	2

Chord	Group	Page number	# of voicings
Dø7(♭9)	All	68	1
		69	2
Dø7(♭9,♭13)	Quickest	12	1
	Selected	40	2
		41	1
	All	68	2
		69	3
Dø7(11)	Quickest	12	3
		13	1
	Selected	40	2
		41	1
	All	68	4
		69	2
Dø7(11,♭13)	Selected	40	2
		41	2
	All	68	2
		69	2
Dø7(♭13)	All	68	1
Dø9(♭13)	Selected	41	1
	All	69	2
Dø11	Quickest	12	5
	Selected	40	1
		41	3
	All	68	1
		69	3
Dø11(♭9)	Quickest	12	3
	Selected	41	2
	All	69	2

Chord	Group	Page number	# of voicings
G7(♭9)	Quickest	10	1
		12	1
	Selected	16	1
		40	1
	All	66	1
		68	1
G7(♭9,♯9,♭13)	Quickest	10	1
		12	1
	Selected	16	2
		17	1
		40	2
		41	1
	All	66	2
		67	1
		68	2
		69	1
G7(♭9,♯11)	Quickest	11	1
		13	1
	Selected	16	2
		40	2
	All	66	2
		68	2
G7(♭9,♯11,♭13)	Quickest	10	1
		12	1
	Selected	16	1
		17	2
		40	1
		41	2
	All	66	1
		67	2
		68	1
		69	2
G7(♭9,13)	Quickest	11	1
		13	1
	All	66	1
		68	1
G7(♭9,♭13)	Quickest	11	1
		13	1
G7(♯9,13)	All	67	1
		69	1
G7(♯9,♭13)	All	67	1
		69	1
G7(13)	Quickest	12	1
	Selected	17	1
		41	1
	All	67	1
		69	1
G7(♭13)	Quickest	12	1
	Selected	17	1
		41	1
	All	67	1
		69	1

Chord	Group	Page number	# of voicings
G9	Quickest	10	1
		11	1
		12	1
		13	1
	Selected	16	2
		40	2
	All	66	2
		68	2
G9(♯11)	Quickest	13	1
G9(13)	Quickest	10	2
		11	1
		12	2
		13	1
	Selected	16	1
		17	2
		40	1
		41	2
	All	66	2
		67	3
		68	2
		69	3
G9(♭13)	Quickest	10	2
		12	2
	Selected	17	1
		41	1
	All	67	1
		69	1
G13(♭9,♯11)	Quickest	10	1
		12	1
	Selected	17	1
		41	1
	All	67	1
		69	1
G13(♯11)	Quickest	10	1
		12	1
	Selected	17	1
		41	1
	All	67	1
		69	1

Index of voicings

Chord	Group	Page number	# of voicings
CΔ6(9)	Quickest	10	2
		11	2
	Selected	16	2
		17	2
	All	66	5
		67	4
CΔ6(9,#11)	Quickest	11	1
CΔ7(#11)	All	66	1
CΔ7(#11,13)	All	66	1
CΔ7(13)	All	66	2
CΔ9	Quickest	11	1
	Selected	17	1
	All	66	1
		67	2
CΔ9(#11)	All	67	1
CΔ9(13)	Quickest	10	5
		11	2
	Selected	16	5
		17	2
	All	66	6
		67	5
CΔ13(#11)	Quickest	10	2
	Selected	16	2
		17	1
	All	66	2
		67	1

Chord	Group	Page number	# of voicings
Cm6	Quickest	13	1
Cm6(9)	Quickest	12	1
		13	1
	Selected	40	1
		41	1
	All	68	2
		69	2
Cm6(9,11)	Quickest	12	2
	Selected	41	2
	All	69	2
Cm6(11)	Quickest	12	1
	Selected	40	2
	All	68	2
Cm7	Quickest	13	1
	All	68	1
Cm7(11)	Quickest	12	1
	Selected	40	2
	All	68	3
CmΔ7(9,13)	Quickest	12	2
	Selected	40	1
		41	2
	All	68	1
		69	2
CmΔ7(9)	Quickest	13	1
	Selected	41	1
	All	68	1
		69	2
Cm9	Quickest	12	1
		13	1
	Selected	40	1
		41	1
	All	68	1
		69	2
Cm9(13)	Quickest	12	1
	Selected	40	1
		41	1
	All	68	1
		69	1
Cm11	Quickest	12	2
	Selected	41	2
	All	69	3

ARTIST TRANSCRIPTIONS

Artist Transcriptions are authentic, note-for-note transcriptions of the hottest artists in jazz, pop, and rock today. These outstanding, accurate arrangements are in an easy-to-read format which includes all essential lines. Artist Transcriptions can be used to perform, sequence or reference.

GUITAR & BASS

The Guitar Style of George Benson
00660113.................................$14.95

The Guitar Book of Pierre Bensusan
00699072.................................$19.95

Ron Carter – Acoustic Bass
00672331.................................$16.95

**Charley Christian –
The Art of Jazz Guitar**
00026704.................................. $9.95

Stanley Clarke Collection
00672307.................................$19.95

Al Di Meola – Cielo E Terra
00604041.................................$14.95

**Al Di Meola –
Friday Night in San Francisco**
00660115.................................$14.95

Al Di Meola – Music, Words, Pictures
00604043.................................$14.95

Kevin Eubanks Guitar Collection
00672319.................................$19.95

The Jazz Style of Tal Farlow
00673245.................................$19.95

Bela Fleck and the Flecktones
00672359 Melody/Lyrics/Chords....$16.95

David Friesen – Years Through Time
00673253.................................$14.95

Best Of Frank Gambale
00672336.................................$22.95

Jim Hall – Jazz Guitar Environments
00699389 Book/CD $19.95

Jim Hall – Exploring Jazz Guitar
00699306.................................$17.95

Scott Henderson Guitar Book
00699330.................................$19.95

**Allan Holdsworth –
Reaching for the Uncommon Chord**
00604049.................................$14.95

Leo Kottke – Eight Songs
00699215.................................$14.95

Wes Montgomery – Guitar Transcriptions
00675536.................................$17.95

Joe Pass Collection
00672353.................................$18.95

John Patitucci
00673216.................................$14.95

Django Reinhardt Anthology
00027083.................................$14.95

The Genius of Django Reinhardt
00026711.................................$10.95

Django Reinhardt – A Treasury of Songs
00026715.................................$12.95

Great Rockabilly Guitar Solos
00692820.................................$14.95

Johnny Smith Guitar Solos
00672374.................................$16.95

Mike Stern Guitar Book
00673224.................................$16.95

Mark Whitfield
00672320.................................$19.95

Jack Wilkins – Windows
00673249.................................$14.95

Gary Willis Collection
00672337.................................$19.95

CLARINET

Buddy De Franco Collection
00672423.................................$19.95

TROMBONE

J.J. Johnson Collection
00672332.................................$19.95

TRUMPET

The Chet Baker Collection
00672435.................................$19.95

Randy Brecker
00673234.................................$14.95

**The Brecker Brothers...
And All Their Jazz**
00672351.................................$19.95

Best of the Brecker Brothers
00672447.................................$19.95

Miles Davis – Originals
00672448.................................$19.95

Miles Davis – Standards Vol. 1
00672450.................................$19.95

The Dizzy Gillespie Collection
00672479.................................$19.95

Freddie Hubbard
00673214.................................$14.95

Tom Harrell Jazz Trumpet
00672382.................................$19.95

Jazz Trumpet Solos
00672363.................................. $9.95

FLUTE

James Newton – Improvising Flute
00660108.................................$14.95

The Lew Tabackin Collection
00672455.................................$19.95

PIANO & KEYBOARD

Monty Alexander Collection
00672338.................................$19.95

Kenny Barron Collection
00672318.................................$22.95

Warren Bernhardt Collection
00672364.................................$19.95

Cyrus Chesnut Collection
00672439.................................$19.95

Billy Childs Collection
00673242.................................$19.95

Chick Corea – Elektric Band
00603126.................................$15.95

Chick Corea – Paint the World
00672300.................................$12.95

Bill Evans Collection
00672365.................................$19.95

Benny Green Collection
00672329.................................$19.95

Herbie Hancock Collection
00672419.................................$19.95

Gene Harris Collection
00672446.................................$19.95

Ahmad Jamal Collection
00672322.................................$22.95

Jazz Master Classics for Piano
00672354.................................$14.95

**Thelonious Monk – Intermediate
Piano Solos**
00672392.................................$14.95

Jelly Roll Morton – The Piano Rolls
00672433.................................$12.95

Michel Petrucciani
00673226.................................$17.95

Bud Powell Classics
00672371.................................$19.95

André Previn Collection
00672437.................................$19.95

Horace Silver Collection
00672303.................................$19.95

Art Tatum Collection
00672316.................................$22.95

Art Tatum Solo Book
00672355.................................$19.95

Billy Taylor Collection
00672357.................................$24.95

McCoy Tyner
00673215.................................$16.95

Cedar Walton Collection
00672321.................................$19.95

SAXOPHONE

Julian "Cannonball" Adderly Collection
00673244.................................$18.95

Michael Brecker
00673237.................................$19.95

Michael Brecker Collection
00672429.................................$19.95

**The Brecker Brothers...
And All Their Jazz**
00672351.................................$19.95

Best of the Brecker Brothers
00672447.................................$19.95

Benny Carter Plays Standards
00672315.................................$22.95

Benny Carter Collection
00672314.................................$22.95

James Carter Collection
00672394.................................$19.95

John Coltrane – Giant Steps
00672349.................................$19.95

John Coltrane Solos
00673233.................................$22.95

Paul Desmond Collection
00672328.................................$19.95

Paul Desmond – Standard Time
00672454.................................$19.95

Stan Getz
00699375.................................$18.95

Stan Getz – Bossa Novas
00672377.................................$19.95

Stan Getz – Standards
00672375.................................$17.95

Great Tenor Sax Solos
00673254.................................$18.95

**Joe Henderson – Selections from
"Lush Life" & "So Near So Far"**
00673252.................................$19.95

Best of Joe Henderson
00672330.................................$22.95

Jazz Master Classics for Tenor Sax
00672350.................................$18.95

Best Of Kenny G
00673239.................................$19.95

Kenny G – Breathless
00673229.................................$19.95

Kenny G – Classics in the Key of G
00672462.................................$19.95

Kenny G – The Moment
00672373.................................$19.95

Joe Lovano Collection
00672326.................................$19.95

James Moody Collection – Sax and Flute
00672372.................................$19.95

The Frank Morgan Collection
00672416.................................$19.95

The Art Pepper Collection
00672301.................................$19.95

Sonny Rollins Collection
00672444.................................$19.95

David Sanborn Collection
00675000.................................$16.95

The Lew Tabackin Collection
00672455.................................$19.95

Stanley Turrentine Collection
00672334.................................$19.95

Ernie Watts Saxophone Collection
00673256.................................$18.95

FOR MORE INFORMATION, SEE YOUR LOCAL MUSIC DEALER,
OR WRITE TO:

HAL•LEONARD®
C O R P O R A T I O N

7777 W. BLUEMOUND RD. P.O. BOX 13819 MILWAUKEE, WI 53213

Visit our web site for a complete listing of our titles with songlists.
www.halleonard.com

Prices and availability subject to change without notice.
Some products may not be available outside the U.S.A.

0901

REAL JAZZ FAKE BOOKS
FROM HAL LEONARD

These magnificent compilations hold over 240 standards of jazz repertoire in each book, containing easy-to-read authentic hand-written jazz engravings. The collections also feature the original harmony, and an alternate harmonization reflecting common practice by many jazz artists, so players can choose to use the traditional version, a hipper version, or a combination of the two! Spiral comb bound.

THE HAL LEONARD REAL JAZZ CLASSICS BOOK

Over 300 classic jazz hits, including: After the Rain • Airegin • All Blues • Along Came Betty • Ana Maria • Bags' Groove • Billie's Bounce (Bill's Bounce) • Birdland • Blues in Hoss Flat (Foster/Basie) • Boplicity (Be Bop Lives) • The Champ • Chelsea Bridge • A Child Is Born • Don't Be That Way • Emancipation Blues • Epistrophy • Footprints • Freddie Freeloader • Giant Steps • Half Nelson • I Waited for You • In Walked Bud • Israel • Johnny Come Lately • Jordu • Jump, Jive An' Wail • Lady Bird • Lemon Drop • Line for Lyons • Little Waltz • Lullaby of Birdland • Mambo #5 • Miles • Naima (Niema) • A Night in Tunisia • One for Daddy • Passion Flower • Peel Me a Grape • Quiet Now • Red Top • Robin's Nest • Rosewood • Ruby, My Dear • Seven Come Eleven • Sidewinder • So Far Away • So What • Song for Helen • Stolen Moments • Take Five • Tenor Madness • Time Remembered • Waltz for Debby • Well You Needn't (It's over Now) • Yardbird Suite • and more.

_____ 00240162	C Edition	$39.95
_____ 00240174	B♭ Edition	$39.95
_____ 00240175	E♭ Edition	$39.95

THE HAL LEONARD REAL JAZZ STANDARDS FAKE BOOK

246 songs, including: Ain't Misbehavin' • Angel Eyes • Bein' Green • Blue Skies • Brazil • Cherokee (Indian Love Song) • Crazy He Calls Me • Darn That Dream • Desafinado (Off Key) • Early Autumn • Easy Living • Fever • For Every Man There's a Woman • Girl Talk • Good Morning Heartache • Here's That Rainy Day • How Little We Know • I Can't Give You Anything but Love • I Didn't Know What Time It Was • I Got It Bad and That Ain't Good • I Remember You • I'll Be Around • I'm Beginning to See the Light • I've Heard That Song Before • Imagination • It Could Happen to You • It's Easy to Remember • June in January • Lazy Afternoon • Midnight Sun • My Blue Heaven • My One and Only Love • Mood Indigo • Moonglow • One for My Baby (And One More for the Road) • Satin Doll • Sophisticated Lady • Star Dust • Tenderly • When Sunny Gets Blue • and more. Spiral comb bound.

_____ 00240161	C Edition	$39.95
_____ 00240173	B♭ Edition	$39.95
_____ 00240172	E♭ Edition	$39.95

FOR MORE INFORMATION, SEE YOUR LOCAL MUSIC DEALER,
OR WRITE TO:

HAL•LEONARD®
CORPORATION

7777 W. BLUEMOUND RD. P.O. BOX 13819 MILWAUKEE, WI 53213

Visit Hal Leonard Online at
www.halleonard.com

Prices, contents and availability subject to change without notice.